GOSPEL NIGHT

Books by Michael Waters

Gospel Night 2011
Selected Poems (UK) 2011
Darling Vulgarity 2006
Parthenopi: New and Selected Poems 2001
Green Ash, Red Maple, Black Gum 1997
Bountiful 1992
The Burden Lifters 1989
Anniversary of the Air 1985
Not Just Any Death 1979
Fish Light 1975

Editor:

Contemporary American Poetry (with A. Poulin, Jr.) Eighth Edition, 2006;
   Seventh Edition, 2001
Perfect in Their Art: Poems on Boxing from Homer to Ali (with Robert Hedin) 2003
A. Poulin, Jr. Selected Poems 2001
Dissolve to Island: On the Poetry of John Logan 1984

GOSPEL NIGHT

POEMS BY

MICHAEL WATERS

AMERICAN POETS CONTINUUM SERIES, NO. 129

BOA Editions, Ltd. ❧ Rochester, NY ❧ 2011

First Edition
11 12 13 14   7 6 5 4 3 2 1

For information about permission to reuse any material from this book please contact The Per-
missions Company at www.permissionscompany.com or e-mail permdude@eclipse.net.

Publications by BOA Editions, Ltd.—a not-for-profit corporation under section 501 (c) (3)
of the United States Internal Revenue Code—are made possible with funds from a variety of
sources, including public funds from the New York State Council on the Arts, a state agency; the
Literature Program of the National Endowment for the Arts; the County of Monroe, NY; the
Lannan Foundation for support of the Lannan Translations Selection Series; the Sonia Raiziss
Giop Charitable Foundation; the Mary S. Mulligan Charitable Trust; the Rochester Area Com-
munity Foundation; the Arts & Cultural Council for Greater Rochester; the Steeple-Jack Fund;
the Ames-Amzalak Memorial Trust in memory of Henry Ames, Semon Amzalak and Dan
Amzalak; and contributions from many individuals nationwide. See Colophon on page 80 for
special individual acknowledgments.

Cover Art and Design: Daphne Morrissey
Interior Design and Composition: Richard Foerster
Manufacturing: McNaughton & Gunn
BOA Logo: Mirko

Library of Congress Cataloging-in-Publication Data

Waters, Michael, 1949–
  Gospel night : poems / by Michael Waters. — 1st ed.
     p. cm. — (American poets continuum series ; no. 129)
  ISBN 978-1-934414-53-8 (trade pbk.)
  I. Title.
  PS3573.A818G67 2011
  811'.54—dc22
                                        2011001948

NATIONAL
ENDOWMENT
FOR THE ARTS
A great nation
deserves great art.

BOA Editions, Ltd.
250 North Goodman Street, Suite 306
Rochester, NY 14607
www.boaeditions.org
A. Poulin, Jr., Founder (1938–1996)

State of the Arts

NYSCA

CONTENTS

I

II

III

IV

✻

for Mihaela

kamavtu

We live in filth, we eat, drink and bathe in it; as we can we thrive on it. We are suffocated by the primitive and the pure.

—William Carlos Williams

Gospel Night

I

WHITE STORK

Ciconia ciconia

Such jazzy arrhythmia,
                    the white storks'
Plosive and gorgeous leave-takings suggest
Oracular utterance where the blurred
Danube disperses its silts.
                    Then the red-
Billed, red-legged creatures begin to spiral,
To float among thermals like the souls, wrote
Pythagoras, praising the expansive
Grandeur of black-tipped wings, of dead poets.
Most Eastern cultures would not allow them
To be struck, not with slung stone or arrow
Or, later, lead bullet—
                    birds who have learned,
While living, to keep their songs to themselves,
Who return to nests used for centuries,
Nests built on rooftops, haystacks, telegraph
Poles, on wooden wagon wheels placed on cold
Chimneys by peasants who hoped to draw down
Upon plague-struck villages such winged luck.

If the body in its failure remains
A nest, if the soul chooses to return...

Yet not one stork has been born in Britain
Since 1416, the last nest renounced
When Julian of Norwich, anchoress,
Having exhausted all revelations,
Took earthly dispensation, that final
Stork assuring, even while vanishing,
"Sin is behovely, but all shall be well."

RIO SAVEGRE

Tamarindo
Costa Rica

Where the Pacific seized the river, tugged
Limbs then torso toward murkier waters,
I turned back, struggled briefly, tore a path
Through the thousand frayed sienna ribbons.
I fought toward scabbed boys jabbering Spanish,
Waving skinny arms like burnt tindersticks.
I'd wanted to cross to the cloistered beach
Where turtles oared ashore to bury eggs.
That night I learned what the voices counseled:
Where salt and fresh waters tumble and stir,
Shark and crocodile sunder together.
I was lucky to leave that turbid bath.
Now I awaken when church bells worry
To recall my shade taken by current,
Riven on the waters' skin, wrenched apart
Black rag by black rag, as the soul is torn,
The heart bitten, as I stumble away,
Too dumb to know which creatures seethe below
And how whitely the body must beckon.

THE BELLS

Sanctuary Basilica
Malta

Pale novitiates flocked the bell tower
To shadow my wife one rooftop below.
Oiled, asleep, she remained unaware
Of cassock-clad boys pivoting the ledge
Until the priest appeared to knell their shame
The precise moment—punctual sinner—
I bumped open the rooftop door, bearing
In each fist a flute, orange fizz daubing
The blistered tar, the riotous mimosas
Two more slender flames expanding the near
Suburbs of hell where she sprawled, naked, stunned
Speechless on gaudy towels, below breathless
Boys, riding the pitch, not so far from God.

CANNIBAL

for Mihaela

Among the survivors of the Donner
Party—idiom's black sense of humor—
Who developed a secret taste for flesh
Flaked between the fluted bones of the wrist?
Who for organs: charcoaled tongue or poached heart?
Years later, in San Raphael, who wept
At night for a morsel of human cheek,
For one finger to gnaw himself to sleep?
In the next century, Jeffrey Dahmer
Ladles a young man's head into a pot,
The water simmering, lightly salted,
New potatoes, leeks, and scrawny carrot
Floating past eyes uplifted toward Heaven.
Chestnut hair flutters slightly like eelgrass—
Who can fathom such inexplicable
Hunger? How my mouth covets your body,
Teeth grazing buttocks, shoulders, each nipple.
How I want to cradle you inside me
As you clasp me within, to celebrate
Our secular, primeval communion.
What can I do but inscribe this desire
Bite mark by bite mark across sweat-glossed skin?
What can I do but write these poems for you?
Ribbon worms know no language but hunger,
So lacking all food will feed on themselves.

CONTEMPORARY LIT

in memory of _____

Cocksucking angel sweet blowjob baby
Who begged me to whisper pornographic
Endearments spring hothouse dorm afternoons
Who failed every course nineteen-sixty-nine
Devoured Djuna Barnes Simone de Beauvoir
Then refused to write the research paper
Not willing to squander their odd allure
Amphetamine darling razored precious
Whose rehab letters crammed tattered margins
Page after page torn from Anaïs Nin
Sleep now sing *sumer is icumen in*

MISERERE

We're bathing together when Alina kneels in steam
to reveal crimped flaps of skin,
drawn shades the surgeons have fashioned: system of pulleys
worked by little metal wheels
screwed into each shoulder. She rolls them with a finger:
the shades scroll: I gaze through her,
through windows opened in her chest, past icy tendrils
scrawling abandoned gardens
where seven unborn sisters, hands joined in a circle,
attempt to sing a sacred
cycle by Górecki or Pärt, a healing chorale
that resurrects starved finches,
lifts fallen fruit back to black branches, replenishes
green in winter-scorched grasses.
Their voices swell through each scar-rimmed oval. O, she says,
look: they've taken both my breasts,
but hasn't God replaced them with such glorious music.

GOSPEL NIGHT

Shall We Gather at the River
Robert Lowry
1864

I thought I saw but couldn't see your eyes
Staring back at me through fingers of flame
As stacked wood received irrevocable
Blessing and lamentation chorused birch.
One barge sermonized with whistled warning.
Fiddles reflected fire, wood wooing wood,
While we thrashed like locusts in burgeoning
Dark outside the abandoned circle, lips
Scorched. Someone shouted common blasphemy,
Another screeched, then swift gusts siphoned smoke
Past obscene reckonings against Heaven.
How fiercely we loomed in anonymous
Ravishings, how high our sick shadows rose
Off grass on plucked strings, raw voices, kindred
Weeping, till we found each other, blistered
Among neighbors, lovers, unrepentant
Sinners, gazing across the fallen ash.

NOTHING

---

the nothing that is
—Wallace Stevens

A man who loves his wife too ardently—
  Jerome argued in the 4th Century—
    That man is guilty of adultery.

I knew someone who hid outside his house,
  Crouched in the webbed & berried shrubbery,
    To watch his wife's nocturnal ritual:

The slow unbuttoning of her earthly
  Garments, the shucking off of mortal guise,
    Then thinning to vapor before his gaze.

He wept among the multitude of moths.
  To love is to suffer, et cetera,
    But suffering teaches how we are loved—

That wife stepped naked into starry fall
  And whispered forth her husband's name until
    He followed the gauzy braid of her breath

To clasp nothing that made him less alone.

MAN IN BLACK

June Carter Cash, d. May 15, 2003

Why Noah summoned two of each creature
Poses no puzzle to any sentient
Breather. The dove hunched on a knobby branch
Misses his mate, though still coos all morning,
And the fat cat prowls the feather-strewn lawn
As if God lay hidden among fallen
Needles. Six kittens caper behind her.
Inside the house, I allow the lonesome
Sound of Vassar Clements' antique fiddle
To trick the wound into thinking it has
Healed. Always this sense of forward motion
Only to be pulled up short like the hound
Blustering wildly against his taut chain.
No heaven but in the momentary
Glimpse of sunlight on iridescent breast,
Or in the note silked on air as horsehair
Caresses gut, sending forth its blue throb
Into the churchy silence between barks.
When I step outside, I can't remember
Spring—the world's hushed now, anticipating
Waters that will pummel the green earth flat
And the one dove who'll fly off not knowing
If he can find an exposed mountain peak
Or, come nightfall, make it back to the ark.

Johnny Cash, d. September 12, 2003

THE VISIT

Bay Pines National Cemetery
FL

I'm not sure how we wound up scuffing dirt
While gazing dumbly down at the thousand
Unfamiliar names stamped onto brass plaques.
We strolled below a formal scattering
Of trees: evergreen, sycamore, willow.
I hadn't wanted to come here to find
My father grousing at teetotalers,
Sculpted shrubbery, clumps of hunched weepers,
But someone had repeated the story
Of the well-hung guy who'd been cremated—
His widow, passing the urn among friends
Gathered for the farewell feast, loosed a sigh:
It's true. His dick weighed more than his ashes.
Some laughter, then deferential silence…
"We should visit your father," hmm'd my wife,
"It's about time I introduced myself."
She's foreign—from a country where the dead
Are spoiled with reverence & begged by name
To quell family squabbles, where snowdrops
Are stolen from strangers' graves to be tamped
Once more in soil above distant cousins:
"Don't worry. The dead forgive each other."
So we're here, fourteen years after his death,
That hard, negative, & enduring fact
Cast upon this plaque under which reside
The heaped cinders of my father's body,
Though he is conversing now with my wife
In a voice I can't quite match, a murmur
That seems to coil up through sap & needles,

It's okay. . . he's my son. . . I knew he'd come.
Why do you think I ferried you to him?

In memoriam Raymond Waters
d. 1993

25

CHERRY TREE

Sozzled with rain, its lush, claret burden drags even
The topmost branches earthward.
Our ragged lawn's riddled with fruit—so whichever path
We choose, we soil our shoes
With oily smears that lipstick carpets. Still, we forgive
The tree its bounty: love too
Spills over toward final arrival in earth pocked
By swollen, blackened, almost
Otherworldly cherries.
Their bleached pits will light our path.

DIOGENES

The water lay flat to the horizon and so clear
You could swim far out past the coral reef
And, looking down, still see the sandy shelf
Tilting below pale, coffin-shaped feet.
Barracuda hung like mobiles in the blue layers,
Cool gunmetal, unwavering, purposeful.
The days were long, and I wanted nothing,
Though sometimes I thought I wanted truth
Until the burning, colorless liqueurs confused me.
I was grateful for their little brushfires in my body.
The days were long, yes, and growing longer.
I strolled through the evening throngs,
The tourists in loud shirts and straw hats,
And dined alone among them while ancient,
Indigenous men bearing guitars and whittled flutes
Shuffled table to table, birthing once more
That one, lilting, Incan melody everyone hums.
In the morning, when clumps of flies
Blackened honeyed scrolls tacked to rafters,
When truth prodded me again
With its trumpet blare of heat and light,
I snorkeled toward families of green squid,
Alert, throbbing, horizontal, lit-from-within
Coke bottles teasing me forth
As if I could unloosen my skin
Like a shirt forgotten on the beach
To be borne away at night by lapping waters,
As if I might join those inky creatures
To spend my days reaching always for the nothing
That remains just beyond my grasp.

DISTANT FEBRUARY

Surprised by the dull clatter,
                    the shifting weight
That seesaws the parcel across one palm,
I undo tape, then peel back the shoe box lid:

A jumble of stones not quite arrowheads,
Grey-green shale I puzzle and fail
                              to recognize
Till I unscroll the ribboned note:

Valentines
          amassed from the creek bed
Where she'd waded, barefoot, allowing moonlight
To reveal each flecked chip, the murmurous

Sheen to thumb grit and comet-tails of algae
From netherworldly,
                    fern-imprinted stone,
From the hieroglyphic scoriations of time. . .

I propped those shards on windowsills and tabletops,
Feng shuiing a few favorites upon this desk
Where I trace a fingertip
                    over jagged

Curvatures of each stony constancy,
Remembering the woman
                    —no longer in touch—
Who claimed as our own these indissoluble flakes,

These hearts of stone,
                    a tumbled cairn
Or modest heap of romantic rubble, almost
A lesson conveying how rough,

How hardscrabble
                    any season of love can be,
This clamor of consonants
Still surprising
                    in such a distant February.

II

JOYRIDE

That road narrowed toward the parkway of Dis
Like a slide in *Chutes and Ladders*, steep slope
Hell-bent toward hurtling cars, then cyclone fence.
I gazed out nobly with the battered Schwinn
Nabbed from our neighbor's junk-ridden garage—
Kid brother of Kid Colt or Rawhide Kid—
Then, cool but dumb, leapt up onto Lightning
As TV outlaws had vaulted broncos.
I'd been bored at the barbecue, ignored,
So dragged the bike uphill to contemplate
This first transgressive thrill. *Oh.* Legs too short
For pedals that also braked the wobbly
Wheels, I whitened my grip on handlebars
And, shrill, rode that sleek coaster toward Hades.
Ears attuned to tragedy, my father
Recognized me, then bolted forth to grasp
My waist, shouting "Let go!" but I held tight
So me and the bike slid under clasped arms
To skitter together down Reaper Road.
I didn't die that week, but broke one wrist
And scraped my nose and lips to bloody nubs
And since have tasted Death behind chipped teeth.

BLACK SEA SPA

Neptun, Romania

Not nude exactly, pajama'd in mud,
The grandfathers stood like unlovely trees
Crooking bare branches as our train curved past,
The century flown forward without them.
A bean field away the old women swayed,
Furrowed bellies and breasts daubed like birds' nests,
A fairy-tale forest of breathing bark
Summoned by spell or tribal ritual,
A final spasm of pagan pleasure.
Mesmerized too, we gazed from the window,
Returning waves, their scythed, crescent gestures,
Their mute acknowledgment of time passing
As mud hardened and only eyes or lips
Or the spark of one pink fingertip glowed
In irradiated, Chernobyl dusk.
Surreal, you muttered, but forced a wave
As we were mirrored in glass streaked with grit
And struck at each curve by sunset's stutter,
As though the hammer still fell on this last
Generation to have suffered world war,
Who heal themselves by interring themselves
In curative earth before the last death.

DEAD IRAQIS

On our balcony, two Iraqis are eating a dead Iraqi
That has ruffled in rain for three days, one more dead Iraqi
Beginning slow dissolution until only feathers remain.
Some plague has infected the city—dead Iraqis
Litter rooftops, and sick Iraqis like ripped petticoats remain
Underfoot, dazed, or remain
On roadways till crushed by trucks. Those dead Iraqis
Are eaten in ragged cotillions; soon more dead Iraqis
Befoul schoolyards and parks. Children kick dead Iraqis
Like soccer balls, explosive bursts of feathers, dead Iraqis
Pinwheeling in air where almost no live Iraqis remain.
For the first few days it didn't register: dead Iraqis
High and low. Everywhere you looked, dead Iraqis.
Then like a poem startling in its clarity: *Oh! The Iraqis. Dead.*

BAGHDAD

—vagitus uterinus:
Babies' cries have been heard even before their births

Last night a Shiite crawled the curb, nosing
Forward her fetus bundled in newspaper
Like a bullet-shaped bauble toward a table
At which poets gorged on spittle and shit.
She could not bear its constant cries, fury
And sorrow washing in waves from her womb.

The war continues. When the newspaper
Slams against the door, sleeping dogs erupt,
So we rise from our dream-house to commence
This business of living, to mummify
The unwrapped fetus with sea salt and myrrh,
And to read, as we work, the crammed obits.

MICHELANGELO MERISI DA CARAVAGGIO

The Beheading of St. John
1608

The Baptist's beheaded Arab fashion:
Throat slit with the long sword, then the gristly
Tendons of the neck severed with the knife
Still sheathed behind this executioner's
Back—the beheading's not quite over yet,
Like the tape loop broadcast on CNN:
Al-Qaeda zealots crisscrossed with bullets
Posing with the blindfolded journalist
Before the anonymous assassin
Steps forward to undertake his righteous
Labor. On websites the tape winds forward
To the crass, theatrical brandishing
Of the skull, another obscene gesture
In a war targeted toward spectacle.
Two prisoners gape from their somber cell.
The girl-servant grips the copper platter
Upon which the head will be presented
To Salomé. Blood puddles the stone floor
Where, aswirl, it twists into the artist's
Only surviving signature, *Michel*,
To confess his helpless complicity.

BELOVED

Romania
1989

She cradles the rag-swathed, 40-watt bulb
Like a hand-painted egg in woolen gloves
With holes scissored at forefinger and thumb
For turning pages in the icy nook.
The library looms beyond gritty drifts,
Past blood-soaked slats and the empty, grease-glossed
Hooks beckoning from butcher shop windows.
Last week she began reading *Ethan Frome*,
A donated copy—some Fulbright prof's—
And felt that New England snowscape her own,
But the volume's vanished between visits.
She hopes Ethan chose love over duty.
Still, she can't bring herself to steal a book;
Ceauşescu won't be shot until Christmas.
She scours shelves for American novels—
Overhead bulbs fizzled out years ago—
Then finds the harrowing tale of a slave
That makes her bulb seem to surge with power
Hour after hour in the cold cubicle.
(A decade later she'll meet the author.)
Sixteen now, she can't anticipate much,
Except to be loved as she loves these books.

for Mihaela

HISTORY LESSON

My wife asks if I'm going to stand around with my thumb up my ass
While she lugs groceries from car to table, then laughs—
The phrase so American, so coarse.

What a comical people we are!—I mean in contrast
To Eastern Europeans—though such
Thinking may be wrong—

Zhivkov   Ceaușescu   Milošević
Her point all along.

DESCENDING MT. WASHINGTON

New Hampshire

"...that Calvinistic sense of Innate Depravity and Original Sin, from whose visitations, in some shape or other, no deeply thinking mind is always and wholly free."
—Melville, "Hawthorne and His Mosses"

One-eyed mesmerist, the ethereal bicycle
Clotheslined to the black SUV
Looped its dollop of spoke-light
Like a laser whirligig—
The front wheel spinning
A narrative of doom-rife prophecy
Over and over, the inky asphalt
Coiling below, vague and unlit.
That flagrant disc, tab of Ambien
Loosing its potion of unconsciousness,
Transfixed me mile after mile,
Viscous fog muffling
The wiper blades' synchronistic
Ticks—I struggled to follow the Blazer
Bearing its silver, wraithlike Raleigh
Along the old logging route, past
Gravel-strewn, upward-slanted chutes
Bulldozed for trucks gone brakeless,
Gear-sheared, and godless,
No hands but staunch drivers' to cajole
Zigzagging rigs from shrill velocity
To mute standstill... still
That reflector beckoned with false
Fire until my eye contrived the seductive
Beacon as its twinned familiar, kindling
Sin-slick reverie on tar grooved toward O-
Blivion, and my soul, now conscience-calmed,
Plunged toward those gates, hell-bent and ravening.

LYING AWAKE

Talkin' bout my g-g-generation
—The Who

The fan makes a tsking noise, like a clock's,
Only faster. Again I lie awake—
Many years pass in the hours of one night,
Each replete with its routine tragedies
(Loss of parents, divorce, slipped vertebrae).
In 1960, for the spring pageant,
My male classmates and I clamored to be
St. Francis of Assisi, arms outstretched,
Less failed scarecrow than living crucifix
Bearing its worshipful burden of birds,
Or the once-dead Christ who woke that Sunday
To find no one keeping vigil, no one—
So, to amuse Himself, He spooked a few
Apostles, gazed once more upon His flesh,
Then rose, bidding only the birds goodbye,
The birds that, generations later, pecked
Crumbs from the folds of St. Francis's robe.
Goodbye, the ceiling fan seems to echo
With its next lopsided revolution,
Like this lapsed Catholicism leading
Nowhere.
          Across America I hear
The stuttered breaths of my generation,
Of those who lie awake, alone, even
With one more insomniac lying close,
Lucky enough to have suffered only
Those common misfortunes of our own tribe's
Devising, so shut up please for Christ's sake
(Try for one night not to think of horrors—
Our cities on fire, My Lai, the Towers,

All our inherited atrocities—
Forget Mary Turner eight months pregnant
Strung by her feet in Valdosta Georgia
Soaked with kerosene   ignited   a torch—
Witnessing swamp candles dimmed their phosphor—
Belly slit open   *the wound in her side*
Her body riddled with bullets   with jeers
Spilled Jesus stamped into mud by bootsoles)
Shut up and go back to sleep's hard labor
In the whir and whap of blades thudding air
Their rhythmic recital   their unceasing
Keening   righteous whimper   abandoned prayer

Come kingdom come kingdom come kingdom come

Now and at the hour of our death   Amen

III

YOUNG JOHN CLARE

Helpston, Northamptonshire, 1806

Not often do I find a nest fallen
Among seed pods in autumn, three blue-white
Eggs broken, rags of rucked and yellow flesh
And hinge of beak still beckoning ants, but
One egg sealed, the fluids of birdmaking
A milky galaxy bundled inside—
So smooth and dry I want to swivel it
Wholly into my mouth despite dirt-flecks,
Lave the vowel-sheen off the oval shell,
Tumble that globule of starling within
Until its unspooled trill begins to boil,
Slips its bony case and kindles my voice.
O then would I sing! I would have no choice.

FIRST POEM

Cobbling together a rough-hewn sonnet
To please the red-haired, Keats-smitten classmate
Who swooned in chalk dust as she read aloud,
"O Solitude! if I must with thee dwell,"
I unearthed a simile in my skull:
Like the eyes of a creature seen through cloud.
But *what* resembled those celestial eyes?—
Nothing I knew. I began to revise,
Still fixated upon that gauzy gaze:
Like the eyes of a creature seen through. . . fire!
Better. Now the flames' barbed, sensual licks
Whipped that angel into "brambly thickets"
Where our narrator delivered a choked
Eulogy that "made weep the ancient oaks."
Keats died young. Sixth grader, I too was sick,
Lovelorn consumptive, bumbling sonneteer,
As each spark from that feather-fueled fire
"Yclept that maiden's name with sweet despair."
She was the Muse whose eyes were *like the eyes.* . . .
I was the boy whose name was writ in air.

GREGORY FITZ GERALD

1923–2005

Like the beret, shillelagh, and goatee,
Even the leg shorter than its brother
Seemed another affectation. Beatnik
Splendor festooned a patchwork persona.
I was your student, one more Young Werther
Impressed by your lack of academic
Demeanor, sci-fi tales in mimeo'd
Ephemerals, the lithe flirtatious wife.
Seventeen, I envied your life, hoping
To sway some hippie waif with heroic
Verses that revealed a Byronic soul.
Now that you've lodged a bullet in your brain,
Richard Corey-like (though cast off by all),
I recall the Gauloises, paisley ascot,
Fino sherry, but not a single phrase.
Bon vivant who claimed affairs with famous
Balanchine dancers, you were unable
To channel the discipline you advised.
First teacher, rage-in-a-bottle, poseur—
You triggered the art of self-denial.

AMATEUR NIGHT

The Dugout
Iowa City / 1972
for Norman Dubie

Whereupon they shed street clothes,
Cutoffs then tees, to reveal
Nipples latexed with gum
Chewed and stretched, then thumbed
To conform to the law of the state,
Nipples pinker now, less nubby—
Bazooka better than Band-Aids
As more fleshlike and easier to peel—
Though spotlights sometimes dried the wads
Enough to make the star-specks fall
When hopefuls flaunted gawky routines.
Two cops waited to hustle them off.
Still they'd return before last call
To quarter the juke for hip-synced tunes,
Angling bones to jump-start the jitter.
Long Cool Woman in a Black Dress
Thumped speakers, off came the tie-dye.
Tease. Coeds raising tuition, single moms
Squirreling rent, a few ringers
Feigning shyness—we cheered them all,
Admiring the combo of clunk and bravura,
Shimmy and halt, funk and chic,
Then rushed home to shabby rooms
To nail it all down in stories and poems
Those early years when we didn't know
That we didn't know how to dance or speak.

ALCHEMY

Familiar words suddenly became strange,
Confusing him—not so much their meanings,
But their characters, the letters themselves—
Some quirk of the eyesight, less a loss
Of language than its transformation,
Ovidian, the marks writhing while read,
Poetry, perhaps, bewitched to *burlap*:
The *p* suddenly tumbled upside down,
The clasps of *o* and e opened—*u r*—
Then the *t-r-y* become *l-a-p*
Uncrossed, doubled up, pinched shut faced forward
Respectively, devilishly—the word
Less abstract, assuming texture and heft,
Rough to the touch, less a bolt of lightning
Than bolt of cloth woven to bind the book.

A

Geoffroy Tory
—in his words

The letter **A** has its legs apart
In the manner of a man's legs and feet
As he strides along.
          The letter's crossbar
Covers the man's genital organ
To denote that modesty and chastity
Are required in those engravers
Who seek admission to good letter forms,
Among which **A** is the entrance gate.

On the morning of the Epiphany,
Having had my fill of sleep and rest,
And my stomach having digested
Its joyful meal,
          in the year 1523,
I took to imagining in my bed,
Turning the wheel of memory, thinking
Of a thousand little fantasies—
Of a certain antique letter
That I had once designed.

THE 27th LETTER

"Don't you ever wonder why the alphabet only has twenty-six letters?"
—Ornette Coleman

Leaked onto a scroll, the twenty-seventh
Letter might resemble a tsunami-
Struck temple or wobbly, sparked-from-within,
Pin-brained gobbet,
                  or some jungly horror
Scooped but not quite sculpted from primal ooze,
Who still prowls Patagonian shadows
Waiting for Adam to render its name
So it might shudder forth in terrible
Clarity to bellow the abiding
Loneliness at the core of creation,
Its mating cry awaiting an answer
From the twenty-sixth letter
                     who jerks up,
Swivels east! west!—but then goes back to *zzz*.

"UR-QUA"

You struggle to wrench free a single word
Lost epochs ago—one with great import—
Then drift back to depths where transparent fish
Illumine pulsing hearts with eerie wands.

I lie awake to spin those archaic
Syllables in my mouth till they resume
Familiarity—
                    augur? earthquake?
I worry the hyphen: there or   not-there?

Next morning you retain no memory
Of such utterance, of momentary
Habitation in some inky namescape
Where letters congregate in curious

Proximities known mostly to the dead,
To whom the word may have meant nothing more
Than *stone* or *fire* or *bread* or *dung*.
                                            Ur-qua.
Desire. To strike it once more on the tongue.

LITTLE GEORGE

How she would nuzzle him against one cheek
   After lovemaking   repeat
     His pet name in her native tongue

Then nickname him again   in English
   Button   doorbell   mushroom
     Fallen wren   magic bean   eighth dwarf

Learning the language metaphor
   By metaphor   until she animated him
     Again   the way Jesus urged Lazarus

To shuffle forth from the tomb   stressing
   The three syllables of his name
     Till he appeared   dazed

But smiling   ready to tether himself
   Once more to this world
     Gheorghiţa   word made flesh

GARDEN SLUGS (ON PERSIAN CARPET)

Deroceras reticulatum

Sultry mornings after our lovemaking
I try to decipher their looped cursive—

Urgent, labored, Mesopotamian—
Gummed on the woven, peacock-flamed willow.

Cowled with slime, the spectral scribes have vanished
Into cool, lavish, suburban gardens

Beckoning pilgrimage, rank processions
That chuff to the monolithic birdbath.

One pious slogger has spent its slick stub
Swirling marginalia among loose

Tassels, the rug's unfastened silken knots.
I pluck that sticky breather from glossed nap,

Surrender its lacquered, exhausted inch
To bluebells, foxglove, tawny daylilies—

Ink-dry ampoule, spongy stylus, blunt nib
That waxed ecstatic for the Beloved!

POMEGRANATE

"About the pomegranate I must say nothing, for its story is something of a mystery."
—Pausanias, 2nd C

I eat the pomegranate for its secret

Chambers tucked in rind   its 600 seeds

Red as vowels   as winter birds in snow

Its enwombing   swampy   consonantal

Pulp   like some post-coital   stickiness

Blunt on the tongue   each terse   tart   syllable

Announcing itself   wholly   juicily

Like a foetal   loamy   exhalation

Whooshed from Eden   *pome·gran·ate*   pass it on

IV

OMEGA

Time fails on my wrist. The little hand halts,
Stuck on six, while the second hand twitches
Like a philanderer in midtown snarl.
When Chico faints in *A Day at the Races*,
Groucho thumbs his pulse against the sweep:
"Either this man's dead or my watch has stopped."
Cathedrals in Malta display two clocks:
One real, the other *trompe l'oeil* to fool
The devil, but still precise twice each day,
Time enough to allow Beelzebub
To snatch a soul. I'm caught in the gridlock.
The erotic imagination thrives
In unlikely spaces. Taxis squabble.
The unfaithful husband stirs now, fumbles
For the leather strap curled on the bedside
Bible. His lover—she looks like you!—sighs.
On my wrist, the sweep hand quickens, then flies.

HDTV

"Mind if I take it out?" our host inquired
In that casual manner in which men
Once asked if they could smoke, even as they
Touched the struck match to a dangling Lucky.
We'd thought his choice of movie odd, Euro
Soft-core porn with some boyish ingénue
Who nonchalantly doffed posh lingerie
Whenever boredom licked its pouty lips.
Some men wore masks. Some women brandished whips.
"Um, *yeah*," I choked, as my wife shot a look,
First at me, then at the undone buttons
Of his jeans, then back to the pixeled screen
As though a warning of coastal flooding
Had begun its *beep beep* fiery flashing.
Our heroine was again unfrocking,
Offering revelers her bare buttocks.
How burdened with desire must someone be
To require release in such lackluster
Company? Goodbye, we murmured, & thanks
For sharing the foreign film from Netflix.
We admired the unbridled performance—
That 42" wall-mounted TV
A window into a theme park of pain,
Its flesh-tones so lifelike, the skin so pure
You'd swear you could reach in to caress it.

KUNDALINI

Eurovision

On TV three women are jerking off
9" dildos slathered with monkey oil—
Some new-rage giggly aren't-we-British
Jump-start-your-sex-life reality show.
Contestants howl as bangles scuff rubber.
Such 'Tantric techniques' stimulate lovers,
Prevent them from falling asleep too soon.
"Brilliant!" cries one as her wrist-rhythm clicks.
Stay tuned. Following the commercial break,
Two finalists advance to hot wax drips.
I've seen enough. Any mixed breed Rover
Can pleasure itself with much less labor
Than these women wield, though video cams
Will wobble them home for mornings-after
Couples' chats. Who knew sex took so much work?
Forget Buddhist scripture. Just love the jerk.

MRS. SNOW WHITE

She missed the dwarfs, those stunted penises,
For whom she perfected each domestic
Art, whistling while she stirred the soup, waltzing
The broom round the floor once they'd left for work.
Now servants ghost on tiptoe past her room.
Why had she bitten that old crone's apple
Only to awaken flushed and lonely,
To bid goodbye to her seven shadows,
Then hasten to the castle with her sole
Suitor, her thimbles, and one cold needle?
She grew paler, having swapped sleep for sex,
And though he still could be charming, her prince
Grew inattentive, except on those nights
When he thawed the snowdrift of her body
To slip into pools of balms and perfumes.
How furiously she gave herself then,
As she'd seen creatures do in their seasons,
Hoping to conceive a son, some Bashful
To cradle at her breast like a straw doll
Whose loose button eye begs thread, some Dopey
Who reeks of the lost, owl-quavering woods.

LOG CABIN

First sanctum of solitude and ruin,
Boyhood tabernacle bereft of prayer,
The log cabin purchased for one dollar—
The ad scissored from the inside cover
Of *Justice League of America*—
Arrived in a flat business envelope.
I'd thought to live away from family,
Catholic father and Jewish mother
Who prolonged cocktail hour with secular
Oaths until highball glasses lay shattered,
Long shards glinting in gummy shag. I'd thought
To civilize the Brooklyn wilderness,
Bear law unto the heathen lands.
                                    Nothing
More than a whopping square of yellow crepe,
"Logs" inked onto all four "walls," the cabin
Unfolded over the kitchen table
Long enough to trail the floor, where I stooped,
Chagrined, inhabiting my foolishness,
Less Dan'l Boone than self-scarred savage,
Murder rattling my bones for the makers
Of commerce, the wily illustrators,
Scheming superheroes, and my parents
Laughing now, urging their pioneer home,
Supper ready and no God in the house.

DOG IN SPACE

Friday nights on WINS
Murray the K counted down the Top Ten.
A boy who loved the idea of order—
All objects having their place in the world—
I recorded each hit, its spot on the chart,
Then rummaged for meaning in weekly lists
As solemn scholars combed Dead Sea Scrolls.
The names of songs seemed *almost* Biblical—
My rapt concentration a kind of prayer,
Though only a Russian dog gazed down.
Tin Pan Alley was my chapel as cheap
Transistors spewed revival. Ecstatic
Cries suffused Brooklyn wilderness.
The lists warned how sinners would be ranked,
Culled from mausoleums come Judgment Day.
I Will Follow Him. It's Now or Never.
Like a smash hit played each hour all summer,
The canine cosmonaut spun overhead.
If I searched hard when the countdown ended,
I could spot the spark of the satellite
Among mute stars, crossing the sky, then hear
The weak, unanswered bark.

DIVING HORSE

Steel Pier
mid-20th C

The Diving Horse in Atlantic City
Spends pre-show hours heedless of the pending
Plunge, nose down in the burlap sack of oats,
Unable to summon local wonders:
Herself atop the jerry-built scaffold
Where she gazed upon the unfamiliar
Paddock of salt pool furrowing below;
Or the awed, human *hush* of spectators
Unlike the effortless silence of stall
Deepened by king snake, rat rustle, barn owl.
The barbed recollection of plummeting
Strikes only as inkling and occasion
Synchronize in a wallop of water—
Then recommences its swift erasure.
Humdrum and soaked, she ambles to her crib
Where only one kind of quiet holds sway,
Locust and wasp, nose down in the burlap.

B NEGATIVE

She only wanted to practice English,
The Korean who plopped down next to me
On the half-empty train to Manhattan,
But her awkward, phrasebook question stumped me:
"For emergency: *What is your blood type?*"
Not believing that someone wouldn't know,
She changed her seat, sure that I had cut short
Her civil attempt at conversation.
Better to have lied. The archetypal
American bozo who may not know
Doodlysquat, shit from shinola, his ass
From his elbow, left from right, his own name,
Who's a few fries short of a Happy Meal,
I know now the answer to the riddle
Posed by the stone-faced, Sphinxlike commuter,
And so—under pressure—of thee I sing.

EPISTLE SONATAS

Salzburg
1772–1780

Airy, joyous, and brazen with distilled
Brevity, only seventeen survive.
Mozart composed them for the Archbishop,
Who did not want the Mass prolonged with lax,
Unnecessary threnody, but sought
To enliven the gap between the dead
Droning of the Epistle and facile,
Narcotic unreeling of the Gospel.
Good work if you can get it, though Mozart
Wasn't pleased to be bound by tedium.
Te Deum. So he labored winter hours
Over each clipped piece, each note in its nook,
Till the sonatas sparked with vengeful glee,
Polished like enduring, lyrical poems,
Not commonplace hymns or prose poetry.

THE TEMPEST

19ᵗʰ C

Each plush box, tier upon tier,
Furnished a stage-side gilt wall mirror
Tilted at a precise angle
So patrons might eyeball each arrival
With faux disinterest.
The great European theatres are gone,
Ruined by war, by fire, by general ennui.
Gone are the stagehands, always too poor
To seat their children in the gallery,
Who cranked the handle of the wind machine,
Opened and closed the drawers of the rain box,
And swept the thunder roller over the wooden floor
So even magistrates in orchestra seats
Glanced upward more than once.
Later a father would tell his brood
How Prospero walled his cave with books,
Or—better yet—how from the catwalk
He observed the anemic chaplain
Tongue a coin of spittle
Off the epaulet of the sleeping corporal.

ANIMAL PLANET

Approaching sixty, I fidget with crowds
Waiting for the light to green, the new light
Now flashing seconds allowed... *13... 12...*
To reach the west side of Sixth Avenue—

As skittish gazelle pronk into the Nile
And crocodile scramble off muddy banks.
One doe struggles for hoofhold on water
As crocs zero in like gypsy cabs revved—

No time for birthdays. No time to turn back.

NOTES

"White Stork": *Revelations of Divine Love* by Julian of Norwich (1342–c.1416) is believed to be the first book written by a woman in the English language. T. S. Eliot samples the quoted passage at greater length in "Little Gidding" from *Four Quartets*.

"Contemporary Lit": The italicized phrase in the final line is taken from the anonymous Middle English poem c.1240.

"Miserere": the first word in the Vulgate text of Psalm 51: also the score for unaccompanied chorus (1981) by Polish composer Henryk Mikołaj Górecki (1933–2010). His text consists of only five words: "Domine Deus noster, Miserere nobis": *Lord our God, have mercy on us.* "Für Alina": secular piece (1976) by Estonian composer Arvo Pärt (b.1935), whose own "Miserere" was scored in 1989.

"Nothing": Jerome, citing "Xystus in his *Sentences*," repeats the remark in *Against Jovinianus (Book I)* (A.D. 393). The epigraph is taken from Wallace Stevens' "The Snow Man."

"Man in Black": Vassar Clements (1928–2005) was one of the world's finest fiddlers. His recordings include "High Lonesome Sound," "Lonesome Fiddler Blues," and "'Til the End of the World Rolls 'Round." His fiddle, probably built by Gaspar Duiffoprugcar in the late 1500s, was decorated with unusual carvings and paintings, including one of Sappho holding a lute.

"The Visit": a *mulțumesc* to... Andrei Codrescu.

"Dead Iraqis": for Jeffrey Skinner. On April 23, 2009, The Associated Press reported that more than 110,600 Iraqis have died in violence since the 2003 U.S.-led invasion. The number is a minimum count of violent deaths. The official who provided the data, on condition of anonymity due to its sensitivity, estimated the actual number of deaths at ten to twenty percent higher because of thousands who are still missing and civilians who were buried without official records.

"Michelangelo Merisi da Caravaggio": The painting hangs in St. John's Co-Cathedral in Valetta, Malta. The word "assassin" is derived via French from the Arabic *ha ā īn*, literally "hashish users," denoting a group of 11th century Ismaili Muslims who murdered Christian leaders.

"Descending Mt. Washington": "conscience-calmed" is Keats' word from "This Living Hand."

"Young John Clare": In 1806, John Clare, then thirteen, bought James Thomson's poem, *The Seasons*, which inspired him to become a poet.

"A": This found poem, altered slightly, is taken from *Champ-Fleury* (1529) by Geoffroy Tory, quoted in *Writing: The Story of Alphabets and Scripts* by Georges Jean (Thames and Hudson, 1992).

"The 27th Letter": The epigraph is taken from an interview with Ornette Coleman by Scott Spencer in *Rolling Stone* #1041 (December 13, 2007).

"Kundalini": Hindus believe that the dormant energy at the base of spine can be awakened through a variety of techniques, including yoga, toward enlightenment. The word derives from the Sanskrit *kundalinī*, literally "snake," such energy resembling a coiled snake.

"Dog in Space": The Russians first sent a dog ("Laika") into space in 1957. Others followed in 1960, 1961, and 1966. The songs topped the charts in 1963 and 1960, respectively. I ask rock'n'roll purists to forgive me for fudging the chronology.

"Diving Horse": Various horses performed during 1924–1978. I saw the Diving Horse when I visited Atlantic City in 1970 for a Ricky (by then Rick) Nelson show at the Steel Pier, but, arriving too late, was lucky enough to catch Cab Calloway. Hi-de-ho!

"The Tempest": The Manoel Theatre in Valetta, Malta, built in 1731 for the Knights of St. John, remains active. Its museum houses the 19th century sound equipment.

"Animal Planet": for Alicia Ostriker.

ACKNOWLEDGMENTS

Grateful acknowledgment is made to the editors of journals and anthologies in which these poems, sometimes in earlier versions, appeared:

Arts & Letters: "Diving Horse";
Chautauqua: "Man in Black," "Epistle Sonatas";
The Cortland Review: "A";
Crab Orchard Review: "Young John Clare," "Gregory Fitz Gerald";
Cutthroat: "Kundalini," "Dog in Space";
5 A.M.: "Baghdad," "Animal Planet," "The 27th Letter," "Contemporary Lit";
The Georgia Review: "The Bells," "Diogenes";
The Gettysburg Review: "The Tempest," "Man in Black";
Green Mountains Review: "Garden Slug (On Persian Carpet)";
The Hopkins Review: "Rio Savegre";
The Idaho Review: "The Visit," "Black Sea Spa," "Mrs. Snow White," "Descending Mt. Washington," "Michelangelo Merisi da Caravaggio";
The Kenyon Review: "Miserere";
Michigan Quarterly Review: "Alchemy";
Mississippi Review: "Epistle Sonatas";
Natural Bridge: "Joyride," "Omega," "B Negative";
Nightsun: "Distant February";
The Paris Review: "White Stork";
Pleiades: "Dead Iraqis";
Poetry Daily: "Young John Clare";
Poetry International: "Beloved," "Cannibal," "Log Cabin," "Amateur Night," "History Lesson";
Prairie Schooner: "Lying Awake";
Shenandoah: "Gospel Night";
Southern Indiana Review: "Little George";
Spillway: "'Ur-qua'";
Subtropics: "First Poem";

Verse Daily: "Young John Clare";
The Wallace Stevens Journal: "Nothing";
West Branch: "Pomegranate," "Cherry Tree".

"Alchemy" was reprinted in *The Darfur Anthology*, eds. Patrick Parks and Rachael Tecza (Elgin, IL: Writers Center, Elgin Community College, 2007).

"Beloved" was reprinted in *Mentor & Muse: Essays from Poets to Poets*, eds. Blas Falconer, Beth Martinelli & Helena Mesa (Southern Illinois UP, 2010) and in *Making Poems: 40 Poems with Commentary by the Poets*, eds. Todd F. Davis and Erin Murphy (SUNY, 2010).

"The Bells," "Young John Clare," "Man in Black," and "Gospel Night" were reprinted in *Poetry Calendar 2008*, *Poetry Calendar 2009*, *Poetry Calendar 2010*, and *Poetry Calendar 2011*, respectively, ed. Shafiq Naz (Bertem, Belgium: Alhambra, 2007, 2008, 2009, 2010).

"Man in Black" was also reprinted in *Twenty Years in Utopia: The RopeWalk Writers Retreat Anthology*, eds. Matthew Graham and Ron Mitchell (Rope-Walk Press, 2010).

An earlier version of "Miserere" appeared in *Darling Vulgarity* (BOA Editions, 2006), and was included in *Wild and Whirling Words: A Poetic Conversation*, ed. H. L. Hix (Etruscan Press, 2004).

An animated version of "Dog in Space," with audio recording by the author, was used in the musical production *Laika: Dog in Space* performed at the Ontological Theater at St. Mark's Church as a co-production of the New York Neo-Futurists and the Ontological-Hysteric Theater, October 1–17, 2009. The book is by Eevin Hartsough, Rob Neill and Jill Beckman, the music by Carl Riehl, and the animation by Kyle Anderson.

"A," "Alchemy," and "The 27th Letter" appeared in *The Letters*, a limited-edition letterpress chapbook published by Red Dragonfly Press in 2008. Special thanks to Scott King.

I remain grateful to the Virginia Center for the Creative Arts and the St. James Cavalier Centre for Creativity for jointly sponsoring a 2005 residency on Malta, to the Fulbright Foundation for time in Iasi, Romania in 2007, and to the Vermont Studio Center for space and time in 2009.

"A poet is extended and animated by the capacities and expectations of his friends," writes Seamus Heaney. During the making of this book, those friends included Kimiko Hahn, Ilya Kaminsky, Nancy Mitchell, Walid Nabhan, Harold Schechter, Gerald Stern, and Michael Paul Thomas, as well as the faculty of the Drew University MFA Program in Poetry and Poetry in Translation. Dean Stanton Green and Provost Thomas Pearson of Monmouth University provided generous support. Sincere thanks to each of you...

and to my daughter, Kiernan, love and light through all the gospel nights. . . .

ABOUT THE AUTHOR

Michael Waters teaches at Monmouth University and in the Drew University MFA Program in Poetry and Poetry in Translation. He is Professor Emeritus at Salisbury University in Maryland. His eight books of poems include *Darling Vulgarity* (2006—finalist for the *Los Angeles Times* Book Prize), *Parthenopi: New and Selected Poems* (2001—finalist for the Paterson Poetry Prize), *Green Ash, Red Maple, Black Gum* (1997)—these titles from BOA Editions—*Bountiful* (1992), *The Burden Lifters* (1989), and *Anniversary of the Air* (1985)—these titles from Carnegie Mellon UP. He has also edited and co-edited several volumes, including *Contemporary American Poetry* (Houghton Mifflin, 2006) and *Perfect in Their Art: Poems on Boxing from Homer to Ali* (Southern Illinois UP, 2003). The recipient of a fellowship in creative writing from the National Endowment for the Arts, Individual Artist Awards from the Maryland State Arts Council, and four Pushcart Prizes, he has been Visiting Professor of American Literature at the University of Athens, Greece, Banister Writer-in-Residence at Sweet Briar College, Stadler Poet-in-Residence at Bucknell University, Distinguished Poet-in-Residence at Wichita State University, Core Faculty member in the New England College MFA Program, and Fulbright Scholar in American Studies at Al. I Cuza University in Iasi, Romania. He lives in Ocean, New Jersey with his wife, Mihaela Moscaliuc, and their son, Fabian.

BOA Editions, Ltd. American Poets Continuum Series

COLOPHON

Gospel Night, poems by Michael Waters, is set in Centaur, a digitalized version of the font designed for Monotype by Bruce Rogers in 1928. The italic, based on drawings by Frederic Warde, is an interpretation of the work of the sixteenth-century printer and calligrapher Ludovico degli Arrighi, after whom it is named.

The publication of this book is made possible, in part, by the special support of the following individuals:

Anonymous

Joseph Belluck, *in honor of Bernadette Catalana*

Bernadette Catalana

Pete & Bev French

Anne Germanacos

Robert & Rae Gilson

Suzanne Gouvernet

William B. Hauser

Robin, Hollon & Casey Hursh, *in memory of Peter Hursh*

X. J. Kennedy

Jack & Gail Langerak

Katy Lederer

Tony Leuzzi

Deborah Ronnen & Sherman Levey

Rosemary & Lew Lloyd

John & Barbara Lovenheim

Daniel M. Meyers, *in memory of H. Allen Spencer*

Wyn Cooper & Shawna Parker

Janice N. Harrington & Robert Dale Parker

Boo Poulin, *in honor of Daphne & Kevin Morrissey*

Steven O. Russell & Phyllis Rifkin-Russell

Sue. S. Stewart, *in honor of Stephen L. Raymond*

Rob Tortorella, *in honor of Paul Tortorella*

Ellen & David Wallack

Glenn & Helen William